# TODAY IN THE TAXI

## SEAN SINGER

T|P

TUPELO PRESS

North Adams, Massachusetts

Sean Singer's radiant and challenging body of work involves, much like Whitman's, nothing less than the ongoing interrogation of what a poem is. In this way his books are startlingly alive... I love in this work the sense that I am the grateful recipient of Singer's jazzy curation as I move from page to page. *Today in the Taxi* is threaded through with quotes from Kafka, facts about jazz musicians, musings from various thinkers, from a Cathar fragment to Martin Buber to Arthur Eddington to an anonymous comedian. The taxi is at once a real taxi and the microcosm of a world—at times the speaker seems almost like Charon ferrying his passengers, as the nameless from all walks and stages of life step in and out his taxi. I am reminded of Calvino's *Invisible Cities*, of Sebald's *The Rings of Saturn... Today in the Taxi* is intricate, plain, suggestive, deeply respectful of the reader, and utterly absorbing. Like *Honey and Smoke* before it, which was one of the best poetry books of the last decade, this is work of the highest order. —*Laurie Sheck*

From the passenger seat of Sean Singer's taxicab, we witness New York's streets livid and languid with story and contemplation that give us awareness and aliveness with each trip across the asphalt and pavement. Laced within each fare is an illumination of humanity's intimate music, of the poet's inner journey—a signaling at each crossroad of our frailty and effervescence. This is a guidebook toward a soundscape of higher meaning, with the gridded Manhattan streets as a scoring field. Jump in the back and dig the silence between the notes that count the most in each unique moment this poet brings to the page. —*Tyehimba Jess*

This book burns like trash on rooftops. It runs the river of me like a ribbon through its streets. It makes great sense. It makes no sense. Like a contemporary Charon, Sean Singer ferries the sad souls of our world, paying homage to their respective struggles. In this manner, these poems serve as portraits. Yet within each one always finds a delicious door opening up into the poet's secret soul. As such, *Today in the Taxi* makes for a terrific intellectual and spiritual companion. A must-read for poetry lovers, this book is also a game changer for prose poetry. —*Cate Marvin*

In *Today in the Taxi*, Sean Singer has accomplished, with remarkable succinctness, an amazing number of things: he has reinvented the picaresque for the 21st century; he has created a poetic form, the major component of which is the automobile; and he has conceived a narrator who is both Spenserian and Kafkaesque—all in stark, spare language as convincingly conversational as it is literary in the best sense of the word. The cabbie with whom the reader rides is a contemporary Red Crosse Knight, an Unfortunate Traveler of the magical and terrifying landscape of Manhattan, a brilliantly sentient observer, a Good Samaritan, and just a human being who moves the lives of others and moves through them, ordinary as any man, or woman—an angel, brushing terrifying and numinous moments with a burning wing. "The vehicle is not just a way to get to the crime," Singer writes, "but somehow to bless whatever the journey needs." —*T.R. Hummer*

ISBN-13: 978-1-946482-69-3
Library of Congress Control Number: 2021953096.

Cover and text design by Howard Klein.
Cover art: Saul Steinberg, "Bleecker Street," 1970. Ink, pencil, colored
pencil, and crayon on paper, 29 3/8 x 22 3/8 in. Private collection. Draw-
ing for The New Yorker cover, January 16, 1971 © The Saul Steinberg-
Foundation / Artists Rights Society (ARS), New York

First paperback edition April 2022.

TUPELO PRESS
P.O. Box 1767
North Adams, Massachusetts 01247
(413) 664-9611 / Fax: (413) 664-9711
editor@tupelopress.org / www.tupelopress.org

Tupelo Press is an award-winning independent literary press that publishes
fine fiction, non-fiction, and poetry in books that are a joy to hold as well
as read. Tupelo Press is a registered 501(c)(3) non-profit organization,
and we rely on public support to carry out our mission of publishing
extraordinary work that may be outside the realm of the large commercial
publishers. Financial donations are welcome and are tax deductible.

NATIONAL
ENDOWMENT
FOR THE ARTS

This project is supported in part by an award
from the National Endowment for the Arts

## Acknowledgements

Thank you to the editors of the following journals in which versions of these poem originally appeared:

*American Poetry Review, Bennington Review, Birmingham Poetry Review, The Common, Copper Nickel, Cortland Review, Court Green, Exquisite Pandemic, Heavy Feather Review, Jewish Currents, Matter, Maynard, Memorious, On the Seawall, Orion Magazine, Otoliths, Solstice—A Magazine of Diverse Voices, Ovenbird, Rascal, Pine Hills Review, Southampton Review, TLR, Two Horatio, Upstreet, Waxwing*

# TABLE OF CONTENTS

## 1

# 2

# 3

**1**

## One-tenth

Today in the taxi, I brought a man from midtown to some-place in Astoria near the airport. He asked me to take him round trip; we got to the address and he waited outside the place and someone came out and handed him a brown paper bag. The man gave the person some cash. Then we left; he asked me to drive him to the E train instead.

I don't believe in saints or omens, early winds, or the pink luck of a sunset. I don't see the Lord's love with Her incisions and furry ornaments.

The vehicle is not just a way to get to the crime, but some-how to bless whatever the journey needs. I use my braking and steering inputs to turn inward, or even to go down the uncertain road.

## Antivenom

Today in the taxi I got a fare from Parkchester to the Bronx Zoo. She finally came out of the building, put her baby in the car seat, and said "I forgot something upstairs." Then she left the baby in the car and went back inside for about seven or eight minutes. I couldn't believe it. I'm a safe person to leave a baby with, but she didn't know that.

I was nervous. Some people live without contradiction. I remained calm though the situation was beyond the job description.

Don Byas had a serpent's tooth affixed to the octave key of his tenor saxophone. Perhaps it helped him push into the wilderness, or to ward off evil.

One sunny July Kafka says he wept over the report of the trial of Marie Abraham, who, because of poverty and hunger, strangled her nine-month old with a man's tie she used as a garter.

## B Sharp Blues

Today in the taxi I drove two jazz musicians to LaGuardia, the singer and her husband, the pianist. I recognized them right away. We talked about Duke Ellington. We drove by Marcus Garvey Park and it twinkled like his plume hat and gold epaulets.

The pianist lifted his hand like an axle and the singer skinned the angles of the road. We moved east, we were people who loved music, who were not bothered as long as we heard its copper ore.

Two-way-flowing matter through mirrors breathing air, Ellington was a beauty. He fired Mingus by saying: "I must say I never saw a large man so agile—I never saw anybody make such tremendous leaps! The gambado over the piano carrying your bass was colossal."

Imagine being fired by your idol: you might curl into yourself like the ear, with its glossy snail and white stirrup, lost in the dark until something familiar beamed back into it.

## BURNT PLASTIC

Today in the taxi I picked up a Wall Street type on Park Avenue near 48th Street. He was going to Montclair, New Jersey. His house was on fire and he spent the trip on the phone barking orders at his wife, his roofer, his contractor, his insurance company, and at me.

He kept saying: "Go this way!" or "Which way are you going?" He said to someone that there are firearms and ammunition in the house. Periodically he held back tears. It was a long 25 miles for me, and I suppose, longer for him.

We got there, and the house was burning. The Talmud says: *Nature rules over all things except the terror it inspires.*

## Azabache (Black)

Today in the taxi I brought two English women from Battery Park to Columbus Circle who told me they have a business making art from peoples' dreams. They said how they *crystalised* the dream into their projects.

I thought of Bruno Schulz who said when people sleep *distant worlds pass across their closed eyelids*.

When Charles Mingus was dying of ALS he went to Cuernavaca. Pachita, a curandero, gave him bitter teas and enchanted creams. When Mingus dreamed, he leapt and swam, across rivers like salmon chased by bears.

When he hatched from a mass of pink eggs, he was a fish, and swam over the bodies of his dead ancestors.

## BACKS AND NECKS

Today in the taxi I brought two women from Eldridge Street near Delancey Street to someplace in Staten Island, at the end of Hylan Boulevard near the water. Then they asked me to wait while they had their meeting. I parked by the Narrows. I could see the skyline and the Upper Bay.

The air moved across the miles bearlike in the atmosphere; the pale-cherry tissue of darkness and the little alleys on make-believe streets. From there you can feel the plasma of waves.

Driving a cab all day ruins the car and it ruins my body. My brain moves away from my body's stagnate husks. I think of the old jazz pianists who died young— Wade Legge of a stomach ulcer or Clyde Hart of TB— their sour stench of liquid through a channel.

I watched the seabirds swirl and dive into black water, in knots and roseate oars. Marrow's semi-solid and yellow, moving as we move.

# DRIVE (DIR. BY NICOLAS WINDING REFN, 2011)

Today in the taxi I drove the movie star Carey Mulligan from the Upper West Side to Park Slope. I recognized her blonde face and perfect porcelain hand from the movie *Drive*. One of the many similarities between me and Ryan Gosling is that we both drive Carey Mulligan around the city.

My whole body was running down the stresses. I hate gratuitous celebrity sightings. The sun was a peach more pushed aside than struck down. I felt completely like a driver, or maybe a writer.

Kafka wrote to Felice Bauer and said he drew up a list of things he sacrificed for writing. *Just as I am thin, he said, and I am the thinnest person I know, there is nothing to me which, in relation to writing, one could call superfluous in the sense of overflowing.*

## Days of Winter

Today in the taxi I brought a Chinese couple, parents of a student at Columbia, from Amsterdam Avenue to JFK. The girl was crying, the mother was crying, etc. The parents sat in silence for most of the trip. They didn't speak English and I didn't speak Chinese. I did offer them a little package of tissues. On the other hand, the sun came out and it warmed to 24 degrees.

A driver should find a fixed object on the road, such as a sign or a tree, and when the car in front passes it, count three seconds before his own car passes it. Then add a second for each hazard—rain, or darkness.

The road is not unlike a little pressed-between vessel that the car pushes along its black bloodstream. A psalm instructs that *It will be as it is said*.

## "Fire Unknown Even to Yourself"

Today in the taxi I got a fare on 19th and Fifth. She was going to the World Trade Center. I noticed after I dropped her off that she left a can in the door pocket. When I went to pick up the garbage it was a can of wine.

I didn't even know they made wine in cans. I wondered how people get through the day. Pablo Casals practiced the six Bach cello suites for 12 years before performing one in public.

I get that it's important to control her sensory ups and downs, on the way to what? A first date? An interview? No one knows which bowings and dynamics Bach intended, so cellists can leave it up to their own interpretations.

One time a passenger exited the car and said: "I like your driving style." János Starker smoked 60 cigarettes a day. Imagine the smell of his beloved cello. He recorded the Bach cello suites five times. I thought of blue flames that are neither liquid nor solid, the quick rust like a jewel.

## Ambulance

Last night in the taxi I drove to the Bronx, Washington Heights, and down 9th Avenue. The night ended driving a couple from 110th and Broadway to the hospital on 68th and York. The entire trip the woman was crying and moaning and the man was yelling at me: "We're not going fast enough!"

I had to stop at every red signal, and the buildings huddled their thick trunks. We finally got to the emergency room. I wondered what was wrong with her. People save thousands by taking taxis to the hospital instead of an ambulance.

Kafka, late in his illness, told Max Brod that *There is only one disease, no more, and medicine blindly chases this one disease like an animal through endless forests.*

## Glossed Over

Today in the taxi I brought a family to Kennedy airport. They were flying Emirates back to their home country. They had five heavy suitcases. On the Van Wyck Expressway, they called and said they forgot a backpack, and it was behind my chair.

I was, at this point, nowhere near the terminal. I went back in the opposite direction. The mother came out at the agreed upon door and she gave me a strange look that was half-contempt and half-apprehension. She didn't tip me and she didn't thank me. She went inside.

As the night's blanket moved across Queens I wondered if their passports were in the bag, or something replaceable. I cursed myself for putting up with people.

Then I remembered the poor fellows on Catherine Slip who would skin eels and have to dance in order to get one to eat. I read the eels can swim backwards by reversing the direction of the wave.

## *Night on Earth* (**dir. by Jim Jarmusch, 1991**)

Tonight in the taxi I wondered if I was Winona Ryder driving her cab across Los Angeles, would I have quit to become a movie star? Or shut the door and continue into the pulp-colored night?

Wanda Coleman said Los Angeles was a horizontal hell, and I believed her. In her letter she said *appreciation* is better than admiration because *people are flawed often deeply, and youth, shining so brightly, conceals flaws in the sun of its unblemished adoration.*

The yellow and blue wagon chased tips from stoned musicians or talent agents. She smoked smoke after smoke as she pushed herself through.

We're made of steel and rubber. We only say what is absolutely necessary and try to get many avenues of solid greens.

## Compass

Today in the taxi I drove for ten hours. I was in all five boroughs and New Jersey and did not get one tip.

Once there were factories and foundries across from the railroad trestles. You could see them beyond the red gauze of the cherry blossoms and their white edges that formed the skyline. They smelled of incarnadine muscle, the folks who toiled there. The streets mapped memories that overlapped, and became each other in the maze. Private and public warrens. People loved the idea of the city from their marrow.

A comedian said *ideas are like mice. You don't know where they came from or when they'll come again.* If I were a mouse I would make circles, gnaw on wood, and pause only when I smelled bread.

## CONFUSION

Last night in the taxi I picked up a woman on 42nd between 11th and 12th. She said, "I'm going to Lincoln Center and I'm really late!" I took 12th Avenue to 56th Street to 11th to 65th, Lincoln Center. When I turned she said, "Which way are you going?" with an annoyed, condescending tone. I said, "I'm taking 65th Street. Lincoln Center is right over there." She said, "Sorry. I thought we were coming from the East side."

I was reminded of Kafka's dream. Once a boy and a girl were playing and started talking about the Lord and Her interest in sin. "When I commit a sin," the boy said, "the Devil comes up behind me, you just can't see him." The girl said, "I see him, too, but that's not who I mean."

## An Imperfect Glass

Today in the taxi I picked up this guy on the Upper East Side, and he wanted to go to Spring Street and Washington Street. He had a blue ice pack on his head.

I crossed the park to Broadway to the West Side Highway to Clarkson Street to his address. For 20 minutes, he was yelling about the traffic, though it was light, as his intensity continued.

I wondered if their wound was self-inflicted, an accident, or something else. I could see how he might make a person lose his composure.

After a while driving eight hours a day, the driver and the car become one. It is not unlike being a person—moving forward on a one-way that is irreversible and pre-determined. I instinctively compute the spaces around the car and move faster—mirror in the mirror— then only briefly letting my eyes meet his eyes.

## Limbo

Today in the taxi, driving a commercial real estate type from 43rd and Madison to 57th and Park I said, "Would you prefer to go up Madison, or Park?" He said, "It doesn't matter. Either way we're fucked."

And it was true when a black pier of birds burst from the building, like fulfillment.

I too, seek to weave a memory from foam. A black bottle opener and the blackest bottle, and the flow of liquids. You cannot know it; you can see it.

General "Beedle" Smith reported that in April 1945 when they liberated Buchenwald, he witnessed:

"General Eisenhower go to the opposite side of the road and vomit. From a distance I saw Patton bend over, holding his head with one hand and his abdomen with the other. I too became sick."

When the oncoming headlights are too bright, it is said you should look to the side at the lines on the road. You would stop yourself from being blinded, and stop yourself to imagine the road ahead, unstrung, and the rubber against it.

## Schism

Today in the taxi a passenger got in and she was crying. I don't know why. We left Astoria for Williamsburg. I gave her a little package of tissues and she went on her way.

Kafka said *crying is especially alarming for me. I cannot cry. When other people cry, it seems to me like a strange, incomprehensible natural phenomenon.*

I thought maybe she was going through a breakup, or perhaps it was a passage in a novel.

Some people think of Williamsburg as the "hipster apocalypse" and others, the Orthodox, know the Lord is there with them. She's pushing a shopping cart full of plastic bottles rescued from trash cans.

Crying literally means "to ask for loudly." She mumbles through a drop of saltwater, but She's really saying: You are worthy of asking and having your question heard.

## Rites

Today in the taxi I brought a woman from Morningside Avenue to 38th and 8th. She said "I'm going to be singing back here...I have to rehearse." She sang up and she sang down, the alto-flutter and the tree stump cut from a hill.

A writer said: *We call ourselves not only what we are, but also what we seek to be.*

Driving, it must be noted, is about 10% physical and 90% mental. The wheel obeys the commands of the rose brain and its taut rituals.

## Divide By Zero

Last night in the taxi I brought a family from the Momofuku Milk Bar on Columbus Avenue to Harlem, St. Nicholas Avenue near 150th Street. We had a good conversation. At the end of the trip, when I was taking the mother's wheelchair out of the back, I thought the father was going to hand me a tip, but instead it was a card from the Jehovah's Witnesses.

When Simeon tired of people asking him for advice, he climbed to the top of a pillar in Syria and lived on his platform among the ruins. Boys used a pulley to lift him flatbreads and goat's milk.

Edward Gibbon said Simeon's ulcer might shorten, but could never disturb this celestial life.

## Doubt

Tonight in the taxi I brought a guy from 6th Avenue and 23rd to West 92nd Street and he was complaining that his wife promised their three-year-old blue gum and how sugarless gum gives you cancer.

His wife wanted him to stop and get gum before he came home and he didn't want to. I drove him to a CVS as he praised himself for his tolerance and good judgment in the face of his enemies.

A Cathar fragment said: *If the world were not evil in itself, every choice would not constitute a loss.*

Who knows if the Lord, with one flask of ammonia and another of tin, deliberately added a chemical, vinyl acetate, that could harm later humans. She snapped a blue bubble into nothingness. What did She mean by injecting that sugar into the bloodstream?

# 2

# KEYHOLE

Yesterday in the taxi I thought about how the job is full of contradictions. I'm both stationary and moving, looking forward and responding back.

When Jacqueline du Pré walked on stage, she couldn't feel her fingers and she couldn't open her cello case. She didn't know *what sounds were going to come out or how she'd find them.*

A silhouette moved across the dark sky, with its coral streaks, and glowed into silver sawdust. In its depth the blood of paradise.

## Who's Sorry Now

Today in the taxi it was a couple on the corner of 14th Street and 7th Avenue. The woman was wearing giant ski goggles.

She said to me, "He said I was the greatest fuck on the planet." I said "That's a nice compliment" and moved on.

Martin Buber said *In an encounter, something happens to a person. It is at times like a light breath, at times like a wrestling match; no matter, it happens.*

The body stays the same, all edge and shell, but the soft part is the anvil of light pushing against the copper envelope.

# Dirt

Tonight in the taxi I got a call from a passenger. A man said, "Who is this?" I said, "You called me... you have the wrong number." He said, angrily, "Your number was in my wife's phone and it said 'I'm on the way.'" I said, "I'm a taxi driver...maybe that's what it is." He hung up.

When Jeremiah asked for a solution to stopping the Golem who was destroying Prague, he was told: *Write the alphabets backward with intense concentration on the earth. Do not meditate in the sense of building up, but the other way around.*

I thought of a night at an East Village hotel when I didn't—but almost did—have an affair with the visiting poet. She was a pair of scissors cutting a silent letter out of a word. Though the Golem has a human shape, you could say external beauty has been denied him. Hillel commented: *Where there is no one, try to be a human being.*

## Stretching Out to the Milky Way

Today in the taxi I had my three maps, my bialy and apple, and a thermos of water. I parked under a bridge and looked at its terminal rivets.

The air was like an archive of ammonia and tree resin. At times the city is glossy with simultaneous alerts.

## E Minor Sonata

Today in the taxi, driving north on 31st Street in Astoria,
a bus went through a red light and nearly killed me and my
passenger.

Hit with a heavy object, some carrion with wet fur is mis-
shapen, red, part-raccoon, and washed in roadlight.

If ever there was wanting, you have found it. If something
was lost, let it be discovered. Dusk's varnish, please swallow
the continent whole.

Earlier, my passengers were making out like they were the
last people on Earth. Simone Weil said: *Attention is the rarest
and purest form of generosity.*

## Uncomfortable

Today in the taxi bringing a guy from the Upper East Side to Penn Station we were on Park Avenue when he rolled down the window and spit just as a food delivery guy on a bicycle was riding by.

The bike messenger looked incredulous. The passenger said, "My bad," an expression I loathe.

The bike messenger looked like "Is this actually happening to me?" The guy said "None of it got on you."

The bike messenger looked like "What the fuck?" The guy said "My bad. I didn't see you."

Once an elderly woman remembered Kafka, who had rented a room from her parents in February 1924. The woman, Christine Geyer, said that Kafka, already sick with tuberculosis was spitting phlegm off the balcony. Didn't he see the children playing below him in the arbor?

## TENSIONS

Today in the taxi when a wild HVAC truck cut me off, I
thought of Mingus and how he managed his rising anger.

Everyone knows he put a shotgun hole in his ceiling when
he was being evicted, and that he grabbed a fire axe to kill
Juan Tizol who chased him down with a sharpened "Cuban
frog sticker," but what about in his private moments when
he was asleep, or in the shower?

What remains is the timber of his bass melting in the black
firmament of a fluid tunnel, and the black rose looking down
on the mass of the earth.

## *TAXI DRIVER* (DIR. BY MARTIN SCORSESE, 1976)

Tonight in the taxi, driving on Amsterdam Avenue, I drove over a huge pothole and both driver's side tires were immediately destroyed. Blocking the left turn lane, many people were happy to let me know what an asshole I am as I waited for the tow truck.

I remember Cybill Shepherd's face when she realized Travis Bickle was crazy. Everyone knows the movie is about obsession, but not everyone agrees if the ending is Travis's fantasy, and he dies, or reality, and he is the hero.

When the car was rolling, it pushed through the steam coming out of the street. How did I miss seeing the pothole? Sometimes passengers treat the driver like he's invisible. Or people leap into the cab with their eyes shut and open them only when they feel a hole.

## REAL GONE

Tonight in the taxi I picked up a guy in Lower Manhattan.
He had been drinking hard and could barely stand. I said,
"Where are we going?" He said, "Hoboken" then immedi-
ately passed out.

I drove into the Holland Tunnel. When we were almost out
of the fluorescent lights, I didn't know what I'd do with him.
The police say to carry naloxone in case someone overdoses.
Then he woke up and told me where to go.

After Jazz at Massey Hall, Charles Mingus was unhappy
with how his bass was recorded and then re-recorded himself
playing bass over himself.

It was as if, sensing his own flabby weakness, he made the
whole room feel as he did, and the wood swelled or shrunk
depending on his mood, and turning sour or full, the body
of Mingus in his blood.

## Layers

Today in the taxi I picked up a millennial couple in Williamsburg. At some point the woman moved her legs so they stretched across to the front passenger seat and rested them on the door handle.

I wanted her to keep her feet on the floor, and not just because I fear germs. I almost used the word "distracting." I could see the whitecaps of her muscles and imagine the blood inside them. It was a warm day and the air was sticky.

I thought of the Lord having to clean-up a kitchen after a TV cooking competition. She uses sponges and cleansers to get it sparkling, almost like a reminder of Herself. She thinks desire means to have surfaces so clean you could lick them no cleaner.

## ICE FREEZES RED

Tonight in the taxi I picked up two 'dudes' from a steakhouse on 44th near Fifth. They were going upstate, more than an hour away. They were drunk. They were constantly grabbing my phone, the wires, and touching me. I warned them several times not to touch me or harass me, but they kept doing it. Finally somewhere near New Rochelle I turned off at the next exit and forced them out.

Now I carry a screwdriver in the car. According to legend, Li Po died when, drunk, he fell out of a boat while trying to kiss the moon's reflection. But another taxi driver told me it's good to memorize where all the police precincts are for just this situation.

Their image was tiny in the mirror as I drove away.

## CITY

Tonight in the taxi I checked the console. I made sure I had plenty of hand sanitizer, tissues, some candy. The traffic invades like a black swarm of spiders' turnings.

Everything witnesses everything else. There's a hundredfold harvest of faces, each in a window, and each window in a death machine.

# Empty

Today in the taxi I got a couple on Lafayette Street going to the Home Depot on West 23rd Street. The woman was about eight months pregnant. At some point the man started sobbing.

"We're in debt every month! We're so close to the edge. I can't do this anymore!" The woman said, "I'll return it...I had no idea you were this upset...I've never seen you this upset before." The man was hysterically crying: "We're in debt every month! And it doesn't seem to bother you...you don't care!"

When we were on Sixth Avenue the woman asked me to pull over and they got out.

Poor lovers, one volcano pouring lava from one mouth into one's other, 'till one unravels.

## Floating

Today in the taxi I brought the famous jazz drummer's wife, Elena, all around Harlem doing errands. Cobb is the last surviving member of the band that recorded *Kind of Blue*. We went to the bank and to the pharmacy. She let loose with some stories. It was as if his music was not alone waking up from its dream.

I remembered a psychiatrist who said children wake up in the middle of the night not to see if you're there, but if *they're there.*

I thought of how his wire brushes made this sound like neither fish nor mammal— but this warm ebbing handling a spine.

## Oar and Petals

Today in the taxi I was at Hart Crane's apartment at 79 Charles Street. I imagined him in his sailor's top and seersucker pants, turning the doorknob, eyes glazed with distance.

There was this shapeless, orange, end-of-day rushing. Then I had a pause at his apartment house, as if we could be wrapped to keep from getting stiff. Crane prepared his writing, but nothing happened.

I thought of the Lord having to swab the deck of the Orizaba with a mop, or She was flying over him like silver teeth when he fell off. She can see the current is too strong, and the life savers too far, but now She is below deck, obviously, and maybe he wants to not swim more than he wants to swim.

## Bottomless Vat

Today in the taxi I realized I had been driving the taxi for four years. I looked into my former life and didn't know where it was, and I looked ahead and couldn't see anything.

I picked up two teenage girls on Amsterdam Avenue. They were going to Barney's. They were talking about Chloé handbags. Then one said, "Did you used to teach?" She recognized my face from my year working as a substitute at many private schools.

I thought of the petrified forest in Arizona where the logs became rocks. Groundwater dissolved silica from ash and changed the wood into quartz.

No one looking down at the green and yellow spherules in the trunk's matrix believes it was wood that is now a rock. Fear pressed through fear into the stone's wheel, as Kafka said *not only in innocence, but also in ignorance.*

# The Entire City

Tonight in the taxi the yellow moon was a coin, and the kale florets moved serrated edges along an orange grid. A citadel on a hill's spiral, no one breathed a note, and a ruin rubbed a fish backbone over a texture.

## Form Is the Shape of Content

Today in the taxi I picked up a guy on Madison Avenue near 45th Street around noon. He was going to JFK. He was on the phone talking about his safari to Kenya, his deals selling a gold and silver mine. The Pope was visiting during the UN General Assembly, so the traffic was unusual.

Along the route he hollered: "Fuck!" then "This is fuckin' unbelievable!" and finally "My flight is at 1:30! I'm fucked! This city! Fuckin' unreal!" When we got there, around 1:00, he thanked me for keeping cool while he was screaming.

I thought of the fishermen on the boat Daigo Fukuryū Maru that moved under the mushroom cloud 80 miles from Bikini Atoll. They heard the explosion seven minutes later and were coated with the white ash of radioactive coral. The radio operator, Aikichi Kuboyama, died of atomic burn.

I wondered about the Lord's illusion, a superimposition of waves separated by octaves. She keeps going up on a loop. The brain, tiny in the dark liquid, doesn't see Her dust when it comes down.

## Before You Put It In Reverse, Touch Second

Yesterday in the taxi I was everywhere: from 127th and St. Nicholas Avenue to 118th and Amsterdam Avenue; then from 106th and Columbus to Canal and Varick; then from Canal and Wooster to Greenwich and Beach; then from Worth and Park Row to S. 8th Street in Williamsburg; then from Williamsburg to LGA; then from the Harlem MetroNorth station to 118th and Amsterdam again; then Broadway and 107th St. to 40th and Park Avenue; then from Grand Central to Grand Street near Chrystie Street; then from Delancey Street to Kingsland Avenue in Williamsburg; then from Williamsburg to Sunnyside in Queens; then from Sunnyside to Sunnyside; then from 68th and York to 69th and Lexington; then from 60th and Madison to 75th and Columbus; then from the Natural History Museum to 37th and 8th; then from 35th and 8th to 72nd and 1st; then from 72nd and York to 86th and Central Park West.

I moved the city around the city. I crisscrossed the intersections. I sliced open the cellophane wrapping on a cigarette box. It's vital to the driver to be alert and calm at the same time. I watched through the window and accelerated up the on-ramps. I put on the hazards. I lifted suitcases. I couldn't even identify some of the languages they spoke.

## Harlem River Drive

Tonight in the taxi it felt like the path of names. The city night is like the breaking of vessels. I counted to four and marked the distances. There seemed to be infinite green lights reflected in the puddles.

We live in a time whose motor hums the noises of collapse. Sparks scattered in order to lift the streetgrid up.

The little shifter was set on drive, the pale lighted interior, and three maps sent me across boroughs. A monster is made only of nerves. The driver is nothing without the 3,300 pounds of metal slicing the air.

# 3

## PINK GLOVES

Tonight in the taxi I drove four women from a bachelorette party complete with their tiaras and feathers to another bar. Already happy, they pushed the bride-to-be forward and she asked me how I thought she looked.

I was too taken aback to answer much of anything. She was liquid, prehistoric, and my little body burned.

I thought of the Lord throwing handfuls of sequins at the party, as if to say, there is no other life but this one.

## VOYAGERS

Today in the taxi I was thankful for all the near misses and sudden stops, times I nearly died or almost nearly.

I wondered about the raccoon I saw on Central Park North, rooting through a garbage can. Could this have been the Lord wading through the black molasses of night, and how many years will Her wandering go on?

## Glands and Nerves

Today in the taxi I brought two women from 19th Street and 6th Avenue to 48th Street and Broadway. Unfortunately they worked with Fox News, talked about Fox and Friends, and were excited to see the new Chik-fil-A and took pictures of it. They were polite, visiting from Nashville, and awful.

Charlotte Salomon, before she was gassed in 1943, wrote that *culture and education are laughable entities that we have constructed only to see them helplessly destroyed by a ferocious power*.

I thought of a trench at the bottom of the ocean, filling with darkness and impurity, what Kabbalists call "offsourcings." Shells crack open like vessels, and loose sparks of light.

Driving taught me to accept people for who they are, but other times I wish for an asteroid crashing into the city from the cold drain of space.

# *Paterson* (dir. by Jim Jarmusch, 2016)

Today in the taxi it was the usual. I only drove in Paterson a few times before, either on my way to or from Newark, or somewhere. When the driver Paterson drove in Paterson, he kept noticing twins and then he made his poems.

A new road might reveal an answer, or the driver might find one, and then he could make a change, and shut off the ignition, and shift gears, so to speak, to do some other thing, but there was a long, many miles road ahead of them, and it might be both difficult and impossible; it was the beginning of a day with promises and cars, motors and ways eroding, to doors, roaring storms, or—or—a song for him only.

## Invisible Screen

Today in the taxi I picked up a Wall Street type on Madison Avenue going to JFK. He proceeded to change out of his suit into different clothes in the car. "I have a long flight ahead of me," he said.

The inside of the cab, neither public nor private, is so transparent that you can look through it and see the world. I thought of Adorno, talking about Beethoven's long waves of bass notes, *not of tension but of lingering*.

People in their own contours treat the line between the front and back like a blanket through which the waves continue. Sometimes nothing emerges, and I can ignore it. Adorno commented: *The music wants to 'stay here.'*

## Purple Death

Tonight in the taxi I knew the silence in the car, with its gray and stain-proof velour that absorbed the silence on the other side of the windshield. The city vibrated and pushed the air up or down, as wind among the petals.

I thought of insects who might seek yellow pollen to stave off their own destruction. Kafka saw butterflies as "great opened-out books of magic."

It's possible, but not now, that the Lord will open the door and suck the noise out of the car with Her tongue. It's possible for Her, but She won't do it now. She will be happy if one day there were no sounds attached to words, and no ears to hear them.

## VERSE

Today in the taxi I picked up a woman with a little girl, maybe 5 or 6, on West 91st going to West 68th Street. When they got in I said, "She should wear a seat belt please" and she said, "Seat belts aren't safe for kids her age."

I'm a safe driver, but in a crash, whatever isn't strapped down will continue flying forward at whatever speed the car was traveling.

I imagined fears of the apocalypse: yellow ants and bacteria coming from the ice caps. All will suffer. Who knows what danger we may have encountered had they worn seat belts.

Once it was claimed that the prophets can command things not in accord with the Law. An old rabbi called it "a commandment which is fulfilled by means of a transgression." They opened the door and went on their way.

## Under the Same Black Sky

Tonight in the taxi on Amsterdam Avenue I was pulled over to the left side waiting for a passenger, hazard lights flashing, which is routine, but a car behind me was honking like crazy and I motioned to him to pass. He pulled over next to me screaming and cursing and then started punching my car. I said nothing.

The keys to good driving are smooth steering inputs and smooth braking inputs. When he left there was a gust of air, like a pause. Alfred de Vigny said "The yelling is stifled, but how can one avenge one's silence?"

## Strawberry

Tonight in the taxi I started on West 120th Street and went to Hoboken, Secaucus, and all over midtown. The friendliest passengers were two drag queens I picked up after their performance in Astoria, Queens.

Their zebra prints and glitter reflected violet light in the moon's grape. They said they were "sisters of the cloth" and wanted to make it to television.

The night ended with a summons because I made a U-turn on 116th Street. You can't ask of the city more than it can give you. When they left, their feathers flew into the wind and they ran after them.

## The Smallest Increase

Today in the taxi I got a millennial couple with a little girl, aged two, in Williamsburg going to the hospital in Lower Manhattan on Beekman Street. The woman was about five months pregnant.

They thought the girl ate some of the father's painkillers. The mother was panicked. The father was relaxed. She kept saying how the father didn't check if that was the closest hospital and how she was responsible.

She said she was at her peak stress with everything in her life and the baby coming. At some point she whispered to him that the girl could possibly die.

They didn't notice the girl laughing at the cartoon on her little screen. The car was a snail crossing the Williamsburg Bridge traffic. I thought of the wheels treading on their own slime and glowing.

Arthur Eddington said moving through the physical world was like stepping on a plank with no solidity. He said *to step on it is like stepping on a swarm of flies*.

## Sadness

Tonight in the taxi I drove an older hedge fund type with his "escort" to a hotel on 9th Avenue. She was an immigrant from Africa. She had a gap in her teeth. She was skinny and had blonde hair. She had a French accent. No one but her could have found him exciting. Looking into a secret world, with their glitter and muscles, I wondered how people live.

Kafka, when he was inexplicably happy, wrote that "I'm so desperate for someone who will just give me a friendly touch that yesterday I went to a hotel with a whore."

It was a senseless night with its sad gold and sagging side-streets splitting off from the main road.

I thought of Kafka getting *grabbed by the collar, dragged through the streets, thrust in the door*.

## Which Seed

Today in the taxi my passenger was crying into her phone. She'd just had a miscarriage. Who was she talking to? Her mother, perhaps. She hoped there was an invisible hand that had some purpose in her tragedy.

I pictured the Lord and Her shelf of jars and vapors, Her amino acids and carbons, fit together with one black wheel and one white wheel.

Every Sabbath the rabbi would remove the slip of paper with Her Name on it from the Golem's mouth, and it would become lifeless, nothing but a thimbleful of little clay cells.

## Neural Housekeeping

Today in the taxi I realized my dreams have been consumed by nothing but driving the taxi. Motions through streets and around corners, or braking along S. Conduit Boulevard.

Kafka dreamt of *nothing but Paris cabs, automobiles, omnibuses, etc., which had nothing to do but drive close by each other, over each other, under each other, and nobody talked about anything but fares, junctions, connections, tips, directions, cambios, counterfeit money, etc.*

Dreams are remote from us, outside our power. They crawl through puddles, they pulse through mud, they emerge out of holes in the floor. I'm in a video game where the object is not to hit anything.

## POWERS

Tonight in the taxi I picked up a woman on Columbus Avenue going down to Bank Street. On the way she said she was going to pick up her drunk son and his friend and bring them back, but when we got there a group of teenagers were carrying a boy, about 13, who was totally unconscious.

They laid him flat on the back seat and put a handkerchief under him and were holding a plastic bag under his mouth. All of them were speaking Russian.

The woman said she wanted me to take them to Roosevelt Hospital. At Tenth Avenue I instead convinced her to call an ambulance. I turned off the meter and waited with them for the ambulance and the police.

Would he die? Would he endure? I was a stranger, the one who could remember.

In Kafka's final letter to Felice Bauer he wrote, "If we value our lives, let us abandon it all… I am forever fettered to myself, that's what I am, and that's what I must try to live with."

## Sapphire Needle

Today in the taxi I reported another driver to the Taxi and Limousine Commission for not picking up a black man on West 55th Street. Then, about a week later they told me that since I had no proof, they could do nothing, and that's what they did.

The car, following the other on the asphalt, was not unlike a stylus in the groove of an unplayable record. How could I prove it, so it was my word against his. After that, I installed a camera on the windshield.

I wondered how Edison felt when he filmed and killed Topsy the Elephant. What was he trying to accomplish when they sent 6,600-volts through copper sandals on her feet? As the smoke billowed, was he just being cruel or did he think he had a right to do it?

# Road

Today in the taxi I wished I had not done things, or had done things differently. Or, I wished that I had done things, or hadn't done things the same way.

I thought of all my faults—as husband and man—concentrated in one hemorrhoid that cab drivers get from sitting all day.

She's right there, but I miss her so much. I thought of parallel wheel tracks in the mud.

## Meetings and Avoidings

Today in the taxi I noticed there was a bug inside the car. It was making zigzags, as if the windshield was an empty house.

What would happen if it looked through, into me, staring at our digital displays?

In this one's life, there were glass rooms, and seemingly no exit, but constant circling…fibers woven into the likeness of a human body.

## INDIA

Today in the taxi going from Jackson Heights to Long Island City a passenger from India asked me if I was from India. Perhaps my black hair or my acrylic olive head reflected in the mirror made him think we were on a double journey.

The Zohar says, "The impulse from below calls forth that from above." Maybe lifting away from his home and weary in Queens he wanted to ask in the rolling confessional if my imperfections were his own.

Maybe I too have been dispossessed, locked in moving forward like a body into this body.

## Peace of Mind

Today in the taxi I got a fare on Main Street and Front Street in DUMBO going to Madison Square Garden. She got in and said, "I'm so late! Today might be the day I get fired!"

We reasoned with the movement of the potholes, the people and things coming from all directions.

The bridge had its iron sounds and brown loneliness, the pikes of waves on the East River, and the solid axe of wind.

I got her there on time and she tipped me $20. "This is for you my friend."

Kafka interjects that *The inner world can only be experienced, not described.*

## Two Waves, Brightly Lit

Today in the taxi I got a Wall Street type at West 80th Street going to Pine Street in Lower Manhattan. Where 79th Street meets the FDR Drive there's a sharp zipper merge and a yellow cab aggressively, but also incompetently, made it difficult for me to turn.

The guy started screaming at the cab, "Hey! You Fuckin' Asshole! Fuckin' Move!" Then, to me: "He boxed you in there and wouldn't fuckin' move!" I shrugged.

Later in the day I drove a family with a newborn baby home from the hospital.

The sky was overcast and mossy green. I put up with things calmly, without weight, without bones....What was going on in anyone's head?

## Look to the Side

Tonight in the taxi I picked up two women at Bellevue just after their friend died in an accident. He was skateboarding and hitched a ride on the passenger side of a garbage truck and lost his balance when the truck changed lanes. He was crushed by the rear tires.

There were no heroes and no monsters, and there was silence. They loved him, and they wanted something else, and they wanted cigarettes.

I imagined some vibrations, the outlines of bones—dark things—the way the song moves. The last kind words I could think of were take care, but they were inadequate, and the shadows kicked over the wind's cathedral.

## Take Hold of It

Tomorrow in the taxi it will be another day. I'll read the book twice, then lend it out for someone else to read quickly, then I'll read it again.

When a prophet asked the Lord about what the book meant She said, *Turn it and turn it again, for everything is in it.*

I pictured the black fire of Her ink and the white fire of Her parchment, everything far-reaching.

Among the blur of noise and chaos of the demonic coming from the city's every window, She commented: *Be silent, for this is the way I have determined it.*

SEAN SINGER was born in Guadalajara, Jalisco, Mexico, in 1974. A former New York City taxi driver, he has an MFA from Washington University in St. Louis and a Ph.D. in American Studies from Rutgers University-Newark, and has been awarded a fellowship from the National Endowment for the Arts. Singer is the author of two prior collections of poetry: *Honey & Smoke* and *Discography*, which won the Yale Series of Younger Poets prize and the Norma Farber First Book Award from the Poetry Society of America. He offers editorial services at seansingerpoetry.com.